# Orangeology Trivia Challenge

## Syracuse Orange Basketball

# Orangeology Trivia Challenge

Syracuse Orange Basketball

Researched by Tom P. Rippey III

Tom P. Rippey III & Paul F. Wilson, Editors

Kick The Ball, Ltd
Lewis Center, Ohio

# Trivia by Kick The Ball, Ltd

## College Football Trivia

| | | | |
|---|---|---|---|
| Alabama Crimson Tide | Auburn Tigers | Boston College Eagles | Florida Gators |
| Georgia Bulldogs | LSU Tigers | Miami Hurricanes | Michigan Wolverines |
| Nebraska Cornhuskers | Notre Dame Fighting Irish | Ohio State Buckeyes | Oklahoma Sooners |
| Oregon Ducks | Penn State Nittany Lions | Southern Cal Trojans | Texas Longhorns |

## Pro Football Trivia

| | | | |
|---|---|---|---|
| Arizona Cardinals | Buffalo Bills | Chicago Bears | Cleveland Browns |
| Denver Broncos | Green Bay Packers | Indianapolis Colts | Kansas City Chiefs |
| Minnesota Vikings | New England Patriots | Oakland Raiders | Pittsburgh Steelers |
| San Francisco 49ers | Washington Redskins | | |

## Pro Baseball Trivia

| | | | |
|---|---|---|---|
| Boston Red Sox | Chicago Cubs | Cincinnati Reds | Los Angeles Dodgers |
| New York Yankees | Philadelphia Phillies | Saint Louis Cardinals | |

## College Basketball Trivia

| | | | |
|---|---|---|---|
| Duke Blue Devils | Georgetown Hoyas | Indiana Hoosiers | Kansas Jayhawks |
| Kentucky Wildcats | Maryland Terrapins | Michigan State Spartans | North Carolina Tar Heels |
| Syracuse Orange | UConn Huskies | UCLA Bruins | |

## Pro Basketball Trivia

| | | | |
|---|---|---|---|
| Boston Celtics | Chicago Bulls | Detroit Pistons | Los Angeles Lakers |
| Utah Jazz | | | |

Visit **www.TriviaGameBooks.com** for more details.

*This book is dedicated to our families and friends for your unwavering love, support, and your understanding of our pursuit of our passions. Thank you for everything you do for us and for making our lives complete.*

Orangeology Trivia Challenge – Syracuse Orange Basketball;
First Edition 2009

Published by
Kick The Ball, Ltd
8595 Columbus Pike, Suite 197
Lewis Center, OH 43035
www.TriviaGameBooks.com

Designed, Formatted, and Edited by: Tom P. Rippey III & Paul F. Wilson
Researched by: Tom P. Rippey III

Copyright © 2009 by Kick The Ball, Ltd, Lewis Center, Ohio

ALL RIGHTS RESERVED. No part of this book may be reproduced or transmitted in any form whatsoever, electronic, or mechanical, including photocopying, recording, or by any informational storage or retrieval system without the expressed written, dated and signed permission from the copyright holder.

Trademarks and Copyrights: Kick The Ball, Ltd is not associated with any event, team, conference, or league mentioned in this book. All trademarks are the property of their respective owners. Kick The Ball, Ltd respects and honors the copyrights and trademarks of others. We use event, team, conference, or league names only as points of reference in titles, questions, answers, and other sections of our trivia game books. Names, statistics, and others facts obtained through public domain resources.

LIMIT OF LIABILITY/DISCLAIMER OF WARRANTY: THE RESEARCHER AND PUBLISHER HAVE USED GREAT CARE IN RESEARCHING AND WRITING THIS BOOK. HOWEVER, WE MAKE NO REPRESENTATION OR WARRANTIES AS TO THE COMPLETENESS OF ITS CONTENTS OR THEIR ACCURACY AND WE SPECIFICALLY DISCLAIM ANY IMPLIED WARRANTIES OF MERCHANTABILITY OR FITNESS FOR A PARTICULAR PURPOSE. WARRANTIES MAY NOT BE CREATED OR EXTENDED BY ANY SALES MATERIALS OR SALESPERSON OF THIS BOOK. NEITHER THE RESEARCHER NOR THE PUBLISHER SHALL BE LIABLE FOR ANY LOSS OF PROFIT OR ANY OTHER COMMERCIAL DAMAGES, INCLUDING BUT NOT LIMITED TO SPECIAL, INCIDENTAL, CONSEQUENTIAL, OR OTHER DAMAGES.

For information on ordering this book in bulk at reduced prices, please email us at pfwilson@triviagamebooks.com.

International Standard Book Number: 978-1-934372-72-2

Printed and Bound in the United States of America

10 9 8 7 6 5 4 3 2 1

# Table of Contents

How to Play.................................................................. Page 1

Preseason – 1-Point Questions (Questions 1-50).......................... Page 3

Preseason Orange Cool Fact............................................ Page 16

Preseason Answer Key.................................................. Page 17

Regular Season – 2-Point Questions (Questions 1-50)............... Page 23

Regular Season Orange Cool Fact..................................... Page 36

Regular Season Answer Key............................................ Page 37

Conference Tournament – 3-Point Questions (Questions 1-50)... Page 42

Conference Tournament Orange Cool Fact............................ Page 55

Conference Tournament Answer Key.................................. Page 56

Championship Game – 4-Point Questions (Questions 1-50)........ Page 61

Championship Game Orange Cool Fact................................ Page 74

Championship Game Answer Key...................................... Page 75

Overtime Bonus – 4-Point Questions (Questions 1-10).............. Page 80

Overtime Bonus Answer Key........................................... Page 83

Player / Team Score Sheet............................................. Page 85

Dear Friend,

Thank you for purchasing our **Orangeology Trivia Challenge** game book!

We have made every attempt to verify the accuracy of the questions and answers contained in this book. However it is still possible that from time to time an error has been made by us or our researchers. In the event you find a question or answer that is questionable or inaccurate, we ask for your understanding and thank you for bringing it to our attention so we may improve future editions of this book. Please email us at tprippey@triviagamebooks.com with those observations and comments.

Have fun playing **Orangeology Trivia Challenge**!

*Tom and Paul*

Tom Rippey and Paul Wilson
Co-Founders, Kick The Ball, Ltd

PS – You can discover more about all of our current trivia game books by visiting www.TriviaGameBooks.com.

# How to Play
## Orangeology Trivia Challenge

**Book Format:**

There are four quarters, each made up of fifty questions. Each quarter's questions have assigned point values. Questions are designed to get progressively more difficult as you proceed through each quarter, as well as through the book itself. Most questions are in a four-option multiple-choice format so that you will at least have a 25% chance of getting a correct answer for some of the more challenging questions.

We have even added an overtime section in the event of a tie, or just in case you want to keep playing a little longer.

**Game Options:**

**One Player -**
To play on your own, simply answer each of the questions in all the quarters, and in the overtime section, if you'd like. Use the Player / Team Score Sheet to record your answers and the quarter Answer Keys to check your answers. Calculate each quarter's points and the total for the game at the bottom of the Player / Team Score Sheet to determine your final score.

**Two or More Players –**
To play with multiple players decide if you will all be competing with each other individually, or if you will form and play as teams. Each player / team will then have its own Player / Team Score Sheet to record its answer. You can use the quarter Answer Keys to check your answers and to calculate your final scores.

# How to Play
## Orangeology Trivia Challenge

The Player / Team Score Sheets have been designed so that each team can answer all questions or you can divide the questions up in any combination you would prefer. For example, you may want to alternate questions if two players are playing or answer every third question for three players, etc. In any case, simply record your response to your questions in the corresponding quarter and question number on the Player / Team Score Sheet.

A winner will be determined by multiplying the total number of correct answers for each quarter by the point value per quarter, then adding together the final total for all quarters combined. Play the game again and again by alternating the questions that your team is assigned so that you will answer a different set of questions each time you play.

**You Create the Game -**
There are countless other ways of using *Orangeology Trivia Challenge* questions. It is limited only to your imagination. Examples might be using them at your tailgate or other college basketball related party. Players / Teams who answer questions incorrectly may have to perform a required action, or winners may receive special prizes. Let us know what other games you come up with!

Have fun!

# Preseason  1-Point Questions
## Orangeology Trivia Challenge

1) What year did the nickname Orange become official for all Syracuse University athletics?

   A) 1890
   B) 1900
   C) 1912
   D) 2004

*Answers begin on page 17*

2) What are Syracuse's official colors?

   A) Orange and Blue
   B) Pumpkin and Midnight Blue
   C) Dark Orange and Navy Blue
   D) Orange

3) What is the name of Syracuse's home arena?

   A) Orange Field
   B) Carrier Dome
   C) Syracuse Stadium
   D) Orange Dome

4) How many Naismith College Player of the Year winners played at Syracuse?

   A) 0
   B) 1
   C) 3
   D) 5

# Preseason — 1-Point Questions
## Orangeology Trivia Challenge

5) What is the name of Syracuse's fight song?

    A) "March On"
    B) "Victory Today"
    C) "Down, Down the Field"
    D) "Champions Forever"

6) When was the last time a Syracuse player was part of an Olympic gold-winning basketball team?

    A) 1992
    B) 1996
    C) 2004
    D) 2008

7) How many times has Syracuse appeared in the NCAA Final Four?

    A) 1
    B) 3
    C) 4
    D) 6

8) Who had the longest coaching tenure at Syracuse?

    A) Lewis Andreas
    B) Marc Guley
    C) Jim Boeheim
    D) Roy Danforth

# Preseason — 1-Point Questions
## Orangeology Trivia Challenge

9) What year did Syracuse join the Big East?

   A) 1976
   B) 1979
   C) 1981
   D) 1984

10) What year was Syracuse's first-ever overtime game?

    A) 1908
    B) 1912
    C) 1919
    D) 1925

11) Who led the Orange in total rebounds in the 2008-09 season?

    A) Kristof Ongenaet
    B) Arinze Onuaku
    C) Rick Jackson
    D) Paul Harris

12) The Carrier Dome's seating capacity for SU basketball is over 40,000.

    A) True
    B) False

## Preseason — 1-Point Questions
### Orangeology Trivia Challenge

13) What is the name of Syracuse's costumed mascot?

   A) Opie
   B) Otto
   C) Oscar
   D) Ollie

14) Who is Syracuse's radio play-by-play announcer?

   A) Matt Roe
   B) Bob Snyder
   C) Matt Park
   D) Gene Waldron

15) Which Big East opponent has Syracuse played the fewest times?

   A) Marquette
   B) DePaul
   C) South Florida
   D) Cincinnati

16) What year did the Orange play their first-ever game?

   A) 1896
   B) 1901
   C) 1904
   D) 1908

# Preseason — 1-Point Questions
## Orangeology Trivia Challenge

17) Did Syracuse score greater than 3,000 points as a team in the 2008-09 season?

    A) Yes
    B) No

18) What arena is Syracuse's home away from home?

    A) The Spectrum
    B) Izod Center
    C) Island Garden
    D) Madison Square Garden

19) Against which opponent did Syracuse record a win by forfeit?

    A) Colgate
    B) Princeton
    C) Williams
    D) Rochester

20) Who was the first consensus All-American at Syracuse?

    A) Dave Bing
    B) Greg Kohls
    C) Dennis DuVal
    D) Rick Dean

# Preseason — 1-Point Questions
## Orangeology Trivia Challenge

21) Did Syracuse have a winning record their first-ever season?

   A) Yes
   B) No

22) What was SU standout Dwayne Washington's nick name?

   A) Pearl
   B) Slasher
   C) The Wall
   D) Dominator

23) Which Syracuse head coach has the most all-time career wins?

   A) Roy Danforth
   B) Lewis Andreas
   C) Edmund Dollard
   D) Jim Boeheim

24) Who was SU's opponent in their first-ever NCAA Tournament Championship game?

   A) Kansas
   B) Indiana
   C) Memphis
   D) Ohio State

# Preseason — 1-Point Questions
## Orangeology Trivia Challenge

25) Who holds SU's record for most assists in a single game?

   A) Rick Harmon
   B) Jason Hart
   C) Sherman Douglas
   D) Michael Lloyd

26) When was Syracuse's first-ever undefeated season?

   A) 1913-14
   B) 1921-22
   C) 1926-27
   D) 1936-37

27) What is SU's record for most consecutive NCAA Tournament appearances?

   A) 6 years
   B) 9 years
   C) 10 years
   D) 13 years

28) How many times has Syracuse finished the season with fewer than five losses under Jim Boeheim?

   A) 1
   B) 3
   C) 5
   D) 7

# Preseason — 1-Point Questions
## Orangeology Trivia Challenge

29) How many times has Syracuse scored 100 or more points in a game?

   A) 105
   B) 126
   C) 149
   D) 162

30) Which opponent did SU face in Madison Square Garden in the 2008-09 regular season?

   A) Villanova
   B) Notre Dame
   C) Providence
   D) St. John's

31) What was SU's home arena prior to the Carrier Dome?

   A) War Memorial
   B) Alumni Field House
   C) Archbold Gym
   D) Manley Field House

32) Did Syracuse lose an overtime game in 2008-09?

   A) Yes
   B) No

# Preseason
## Orangeology Trivia Challenge

**1-Point Questions**

33) How many seasons in school history have the Orange gone undefeated at home?

   A) 12
   B) 17
   C) 21
   D) 24

34) How many times has SU men's basketball team been selected national champion by the Helms Foundation?

   A) 0
   B) 1
   C) 2
   D) 4

35) Did any team score 100 or more points against Syracuse in a regulation game during the 2008-09 season?

   A) Yes
   B) No

36) How many times has Syracuse led the nation in scoring offense?

   A) 0
   B) 1
   C) 3
   D) 4

## Preseason — 1-Point Questions
### Orangeology Trivia Challenge

37) Which player holds the record for most points scored in a single game against Syracuse?

   A) Patrick Ewing
   B) David Robinson
   C) Julius Erving
   D) Calvin Murphy

38) Has Syracuse ever won back-to-back Big East Tournament Titles?

   A) Yes
   B) No

39) What is the nickname of the student pep group at the Carrier Dome?

   A) SU Crazies
   B) Orange Nation
   C) Block O
   D) Otto's Army

40) How many Syracuse players have a jersey number retired in their honor?

   A) 0
   B) 4
   C) 9
   D) 12

# Preseason — 1-Point Questions
## Orangeology Trivia Challenge

41) How many all-time NCAA Tournament National Championships has Syracuse won?

   A) 0
   B) 1
   C) 2
   D) 4

42) Since 1900, which is the only season Syracuse did not play basketball?

   A) 1917-18
   B) 1941-42
   C) 1943-44
   D) 1956-57

43) Who was the Orange's first-ever opponent at the Carrier Dome?

   A) Pittsburgh
   B) Xavier
   C) Delaware
   D) Columbia

44) In the 2008-09 season, did Syracuse go undefeated at home in conference play?

   A) Yes
   B) No

*Syracuse Orange Basketball*

## Preseason — 1-Point Questions
### Orangeology Trivia Challenge

45) Who holds SU's record for career blocks?

   A) Craig Forth
   B) Jeremy McNeil
   C) Rony Seikaly
   D) Etan Thomas

46) How many Syracuse players have been named consensus All-American?

   A) 7
   B) 9
   C) 14
   D) 18

47) What are the most losses in a season by Syracuse at the Carrier Dome?

   A) 4
   B) 6
   C) 7
   D) 9

48) Who holds Syracuse's record for most points scored in a single game?

   A) Greg Kohls
   B) Adrian Autry
   C) Bill Smith
   D) Gerry McNamara

## Preseason — 1-Point Questions
### Orangeology Trivia Challenge

49) Does Syracuse have an all-time winning record in overtime games?

   A) Yes
   B) No

50) What year did Syracuse celebrate its first-ever victory over Georgetown?

   A) 1930
   B) 1941
   C) 1948
   D) 1954

## Preseason — Cool Fact

### Orangeology Trivia Challenge

The name Jim Brown is synonymous with Syracuse football and the Cleveland Browns. He is considered one of the best NFL running backs of all time. However, Brown was a natural athlete who could excel at any sport. He lettered in four sports at Syracuse including two letters in basketball. Jim Brown played for the Orange basketball team his sophomore and junior years. Brown averaged 15.0 points per game his sophomore year and was the second leading scorer on the team with 314 points. He averaged 11.3 points per game his junior year and scored 249 points for a career total of 563. Brown was considered a brutal rebounder, but rebounds were not an official stat until his senior year. He did not play basketball his senior year because of an unwritten rule that limited each team to two black starters. Vinnie Cohen and Manny Breland were on the team and would take those two spots. Many believe Syracuse may have won the NCAA Championship in 1957 had Brown played basketball his senior year.

## Preseason Answer Key
### Orangeology Trivia Challenge

1) D – 2004 (Men's teams were commonly referred to as the Orangemen shortly after 1890 and women's teams were referred to as the Orangewomen. The school made an official decision in 2004 to refer to all varsity teams as the Orange.)
2) D – Orange (This color was adopted in 1890 after a committee found the single color to not be an official color of any other school.)
3) B – Carrier Dome (Opened on Sept. 20, 1980, with a construction cost of $26.8 million.)
4) A – 0 (The Naismith Trophy was first presented to the National Player of the Year in 1969. No Syracuse player has won the award to date.)
5) C – "Down, Down the Field" (The song was written by C. Harold Lewis in 1914.)
6) D – 2008 (Carmelo Anthony was a member of the USA team that won gold in the 2008 Beijing Olympics.)
7) C – 4 (1975, 1987, 1996, and 2003)
8) C – Jim Boeheim (He has coached the Orange for 33 seasons, from 1976-09.)
9) B – 1979 (Syracuse was a founding member of the Big East, which was formed on May 31, 1979.)
10) A – 1908 (The Orange beat Williams college 25-21 in their first-ever overtime game on Jan. 24, 1908.)

## Preseason Answer Key
### Orangeology Trivia Challenge

11) D – Paul Harris (He led the team with 298 total rebounds [89 offensive and 209 defensive].)
12) A – True (The Dome has an official capacity of 49,250.)
13) B – Otto (Otto the Orange was officially adopted as Syracuse's mascot in 1995.)
14) C – Matt Park (He has been the play-by-play announcer since the 2003-04 season.)
15) D – Cincinnati (Syracuse has a 4-2 all-time record against the Bearcats for a .667 winning percentage.)
16) B – 1901 (Syracuse lost 8-23 to Rensselaer Polytechnic Institute [RPI] on Jan. 5, 1901.)
17) A – Yes (The Orange scored 3,046 points as a team in 2008-09.)
18) D – Madison Square Garden (Syracuse first played at the Garden in 1939 and has an all-time record of 85-77 at MSG [including tournament games].)
19) C – Williams (The Ephs were dissatisfied with the officiating and left the court with the game tied at 17. This is the only win by forfeit for SU.)
20) A – Dave Bing (He was named consensus All-American in 1966.)
21) B – No (The Orange finished the 1900-01 season with a 2-2 record for a .500 winning percentage.)

## Preseason Answer Key
### Orangeology Trivia Challenge

22) A – Pearl (Dwayne "Pearl" Washington got his nickname in reference to Earl "the Pearl" Monroe.)
23) D – Jim Boeheim (He has led Syracuse to 799 wins since the 1976-77 season.)
24) B – Indiana (The Orange lost 73-74 to the Hoosiers in the 1987 championship game.)
25) C – Sherman Douglas (He recorded 22 assists against Providence on Jan. 28, 1989 [Syracuse 100, Providence 96].)
26) A – 1913-14 (The Orange finished 12-0 and outscored their opponents by an average of 13 points per game.)
27) C – 10 years (Syracuse played in the NCAA Tournament every year from 1983-92. They had a record of 16-10 during the span for a .615 winning percentage.)
28) B – 3 (SU finished 26-4 in the 1976-77, 1978-79, and 1979-80 seasons.)
29) C – 149 (The last time SU scored 100 or more points was against Connecticut on Dec. 12, 2009 [Syracuse 127, UConn 117].)
30) D – St. John's (The Orange beat the Red Storm 87-58.)

# Preseason — Answer Key
## Orangeology Trivia Challenge

31) D – Manley Field House (SU played here from the 1962-63 season through the 1979-80 season.)

32) B – No (The Orange won all five overtime games played in 2008-09 [Kansas, Georgetown, Marquette, Connecticut, and West Virginia].)

33) C – 21 (The 2002-03 season was the last time Syracuse went undefeated at home [17-0].)

34) C – 2 (The Helms Foundation was founded in 1936 and retroactively selected national champions back to 1901. The group selected SU as national champions for the 1917-18 and 1925-26 seasons.)

35) A – Yes (Syracuse lost 94-100 to Providence on Jan. 28, 2009 and 85-102 to Villanova on Feb. 7, 2009.)

36) B – 1 (The Orange led the nation in scoring in 1966 with 99.0 points per game.)

37) D – Calvin Murphy (He scored 68 against the Orange for the Niagara Purple Eagles on Dec. 7, 1968 [Syracuse 110, Niagara 118].)

38) A – Yes (SU won the Big East Tournament in 2005 and again in 2006. Syracuse was also Tournament Champions in 1981, 1988, and 1992.)

## Preseason — Answer Key
### Orangeology Trivia Challenge

39) D – Otto's Army (The group was officially recognized as an organization by the student association in 2006.)
40) C – 9 (Ron Seikaly [#4], Vic Hanson [#8], Billy Gabor [#17], Wimeth Diat-Singh [#19], Sherman Douglas [#20], Dave Bing [#22], Billy Ownes [#30], Dwayne Washington [#31], and Derrick Coleman [#44])
41) B – 1 (The Orange won the 2003 NCAA Tournament Championship game [Syracuse 81, Kansas 78].)
42) C – 1943-44 (It is the only season the Orange did not play basketball since 1900.)
43) D – Columbia (Syracuse beat Columbia 108-81 on Nov. 29, 1980, in the inaugural game at the Carrier Dome.)
44) B – No (The Orange had a record of 7-2 at home in conference play.)
45) D – Etan Thomas (He recorded 424 career blocks from 1996-2000.)
46) B – 9 (Dave Bing [1966], Dwayne Washington [1985], Ron Seikaly [1988], Sherman Douglas [1989], Derrick Coleman [1990], Billy Owens [1991], John Wallace [1996], Carmelo Anthony [2003], and Hakim Warrick [2005])

# Preseason Answer Key
## Orangeology Trivia Challenge

47) C – 7 (The Orange lost seven home games in the 1998-99 season.)
48) C – Bill Smith (He scored 47 points against Lafayette on March 14, 1971.)
49) A – Yes (Syracuse is 59-37 all-time in overtime games for a .615 winning percentage.)
50) A – 1930 (The Orange beat the Hoyas 40-18 in their first-ever meeting on Feb. 15, 1930.)

Note: All answers valid as of the end of the 2008-09 season, unless otherwise indicated in the question itself.

# Regular Season — 2-Point Questions
## Orangeology Trivia Challenge

1) How many times has Syracuse won by 60 or more points?

   A) 3
   B) 6
   C) 8
   D) 12

Answers begin on page 37

2) Which Syracuse player led the team in assists in the 2008-09 season?

   A) Eric Devendorf
   B) Andy Rautins
   C) Jonny Flynn
   D) Paul Harris

3) Which Syracuse head coach had the second longest tenure?

   A) Lewis Andreas
   B) Roy Danforth
   C) Marc Guley
   D) Edmund Dollard

4) How many decades has Syracuse won at least 225 games?

   A) 0
   B) 1
   C) 3
   D) 5

# Regular Season — 2-Point Questions
## Orangeology Trivia Challenge

5) What was the name of the first athletic conference to which Syracuse belonged?

    A) New York Basketball League
    B) Northeast Athletic Conference
    C) New England Conference
    D) Eastern College Athletic Conference

6) Has Syracuse ever played 40 or more games in a single season?

    A) Yes
    B) No

7) Which player holds the record for most rebounds against Syracuse in a single game?

    A) Alonzo Mourning
    B) Patrick Ewing
    C) Hasheem Thabeet
    D) Julius Erving

8) What is SU's largest-ever margin of victory over an opponent under Coach Jim Boeheim?

    A) 46 points
    B) 51 points
    C) 57 points
    D) 59 points

# Regular Season / 2-Point Questions
## Orangeology Trivia Challenge

9) What is the best AP-ranked team an unranked Syracuse team has ever beaten?

    A) 1
    B) 2
    C) 4
    D) 5

10) Has Syracuse ever lost to any of the U.S. Service Academies?

    A) Yes
    B) No

11) What is Syracuse's all-time winning percentage against Georgetown?

    A) .491
    B) .520
    C) .543
    D) .602

12) Which non-conference opponent has Syracuse played the most number of times?

    A) Penn State
    B) Niagara
    C) Boston College
    D) Colgate

# Regular Season — 2-Point Questions
## Orangeology Trivia Challenge

13) Syracuse is undefeated in games having three or more overtimes.

   A) True
   B) False

14) Who holds Syracuse's career record for most points scored?

   A) Greg Kohls
   B) Gerry McNamara
   C) Lawrence Moten
   D) Derrick Coleman

15) What is SU's single-game record for the most fouls committed as a team?

   A) 21
   B) 29
   C) 36
   D) 42

16) Which team handed Syracuse its worst loss ever?

   A) NYU
   B) Penn State
   C) LaSalle
   D) Kentucky

# Regular Season — 2-Point Questions
## Orangeology Trivia Challenge

17) To how many consecutive NCAA Tournaments did Roy Danforth coach Syracuse?

   A) 2
   B) 4
   C) 5
   D) 7

18) In the 2008-09 regular season, what were the fewest points Syracuse allowed in a single game?

   A) 44
   B) 48
   C) 51
   D) 57

19) What is SU's longest winning streak in the Syracuse-Georgetown series?

   A) 4 games
   B) 6 games
   C) 8 games
   D) 11 games

20) Have the Orange won 75 or more NCAA Tournament games?

   A) Yes
   B) No

## Regular Season — 2-Point Questions
### Orangeology Trivia Challenge

21) How many times has Jim Boeheim been named Big East Coach of the Year?

    A) 0
    B) 1
    C) 3
    D) 5

22) How many all-time AP Top-10 finishes does Syracuse have?

    A) 8
    B) 10
    C) 12
    D) 15

23) Who was the first Syracuse player to be named Big East Freshman of the Year?

    A) Derrick Coleman
    B) Lawrence Moten
    C) Carmelo Anthony
    D) Dwayne Washington

24) What is SU's all-time record for most points allowed in a single half?

    A) 57
    B) 61
    C) 65
    D) 69

# Regular Season — 2-Point Questions
## Orangeology Trivia Challenge

25) Which SU head coach has the second most career wins?

   A) Lewis Andreas
   B) Fred Lewis
   C) Roy Danforth
   D) John A.R. Scott

26) Did the Orange have a game in the 2008-09 season in which they scored fewer than 50 points?

   A) Yes
   B) No

27) How many team turnovers did the Orange commit in the 2008-09 season?

   A) 540
   B) 583
   C) 601
   D) 629

28) What is Syracuse's individual record for most rebounds in a single game?

   A) 29
   B) 31
   C) 34
   D) 37

# Regular Season — 2-Point Questions
## Orangeology Trivia Challenge

29) How many points did SU score in the sixth overtime against UConn in the 2009 Big East Tournament?

   A) 8
   B) 12
   C) 15
   D) 17

30) What is SU's all-time record for consecutive winning seasons?

   A) 21
   B) 25
   C) 30
   D) 39

31) Who was Syracuse's first-ever NCAA Tournament opponent?

   A) Connecticut
   B) Lafayette
   C) North Carolina
   D) Davidson

32) How many times have Syracuse players won Big East Player of the Year?

   A) 1
   B) 3
   C) 5
   D) 8

# Regular Season — 2-Point Questions
## Orangeology Trivia Challenge

33) What is Syracuse's team record for most three-pointers made in a single game?

　　A) 11
　　B) 13
　　C) 15
　　D) 18

34) How many times has Syracuse played in the Postseason NIT Tournament?

　　A) 9
　　B) 12
　　C) 14
　　D) 17

35) How many points was SU's largest-ever loss to Georgetown?

　　A) 27
　　B) 30
　　C) 34
　　D) 38

36) Who holds SU's record for most consecutive games scoring in double figures?

　　A) John Wallace
　　B) Hakim Warrick
　　C) Dave Bing
　　D) Lawrence Moten

# Regular Season — 2-Point Questions
## Orangeology Trivia Challenge

37) Who led the Orange in free-throw percentage in the 2008-09 season (minimum 50 attempts)?

   A)  Jonny Flynn
   B)  Arinze Onuaku
   C)  Paul Harris
   D)  Eric Devendorf

38) How many times have Syracuse players been named to the All-NCAA Final Four Team?

   A)  5
   B)  7
   C)  9
   D)  11

39) Has any Syracuse player ever recorded 100 or more steals in a single season?

   A)  Yes
   B)  No

40) Which season did the Orange first record 20 wins?

   A)  1945-46
   B)  1958-59
   C)  1963-64
   D)  1969-70

# Regular Season — 2-Point Questions
## Orangeology Trivia Challenge

41) Against which current conference opponent does Syracuse have the most all-time wins?

    A) Connecticut
    B) Georgetown
    C) St. John's
    D) Pittsburgh

42) Which team did SU play in the first round of the 2009 NCAA Tournament?

    A) Arizona State
    B) George Mason
    C) Stephen F. Austin
    D) Baylor

43) Who holds Syracuse's record for most games played in a career?

    A) Rudy Hackett
    B) Derrick Coleman
    C) Otis Hill
    D) Gerry McNamara

44) What are the most consecutive Big East Regular Season titles the Orange have won?

    A) 2
    B) 3
    C) 4
    D) 5

# Regular Season — 2-Point Questions
## Orangeology Trivia Challenge

45) Has a Syracuse player ever led the nation in scoring?

   A) Yes
   B) No

46) Who is the only Syracuse player to score 40 or more points at the Carrier Dome?

   A) Carmelo Anthony
   B) Erich Santifer
   C) Gene Waldron
   D) Matt Roe

47) In the 2008-09 season, how many Syracuse players averaged 10 or more points per game?

   A) 1
   B) 3
   C) 5
   D) 7

48) Which non-conference opponent has the most all-time wins against Syracuse?

   A) Colgate
   B) Penn State
   C) Canisius
   D) Temple

## Regular Season — 2-Point Questions
### Orangeology Trivia Challenge

49) What season did Syracuse win its first-ever regular-season Big East title?

　　A) 1979-80
　　B) 1984-85
　　C) 1987-88
　　D) 1990-91

50) Who was Syracuse's opponent both times they appeared in the Jimmy V Classic?

　　A) Arizona
　　B) Michigan State
　　C) Memphis
　　D) Oklahoma State

# Regular Season    Cool Fact
## Orangeology Trivia Challenge

Choosing a mascot can prove to be a difficult task for a school. Syracuse is no exception. The first mascot at SU was the Saltine Warrior. This American Indian figure was born through a hoax published in the school newspaper. A costumed Saltine Warrior first appeared at an athletic event in the mid-1950s. Due to pressure from American Indian groups, the university decided to choose a different mascot to represent the school. A Roman gladiator had a very brief and unpopular stint as mascot in 1978. Following the gladiator many attempts to find a mascot were made. Otto the Orange appeared in the early 1980s, but was not officially adopted by the school. *Sports Illustrated* even wrote an article in 1984 describing the search and offering some ideas of its own. The school Chancellor formed a committee in 1995 to put an end to the search for a mascot. The committee considered the option of a lion or wolf before deciding on the Orange. Otto has been appearing at SU sporting events ever since.

# Regular Season Answer Key
## Orangeology Trivia Challenge

1) B – 6 (The most recent 60+ point win was when SU beat American 127-67 on Dec. 2, 1964.)
2) C – Jonny Flynn (He led the team with 254 assists [6.7 per game].)
3) A – Lewis Andreas (He coached SU for 26 seasons from the 1924-25 season until the 1949-50 season.)
4) C – 3 (Syracuse won 243 games in the 1980s, 261 in the 1990s, and 250 in the 2000s.)
5) D – Eastern College Athletic Conference (Syracuse is still an affiliate member of this 321 member conference, which includes 90 Division I schools.)
6) B – No (SU played 38 games in a season two different times [1986-87 and 1988-89].)
7) D – Julius Erving (He recorded 32 rebounds for Massachusetts on Feb. 22, 1971 [Syracuse 71, Massachusetts 86].)
8) C – 57 points (SU beat C.W. Post 129-72 on Dec. 11, 1989.)
9) A – 1 (An unranked Syracuse beat top ranked Connecticut 86-84 on March 9, 2006 in the second round of the Big East Tournament.)
10) A – Yes (Syracuse has an all-time record of 19-11 against Army, 6-2 against Navy, and has yet to play Air Force.)
11) C – .543 (Syracuse is 44-37 all-time against Georgetown.)

# Regular Season
## Orangeology Trivia Challenge

Answer Key

12) D – Colgate (Syracuse has played Colgate 161 times and has a 116-45 all-time record against the Raiders.)
13) A – True (SU is 4-0 in games of three or more overtimes.)
14) C – Lawrence Moten (He scored 2,334 points for the Orange from 1991-95.)
15) C – 36 (Syracuse committed 36 personal fouls against Sienna on Jan. 17, 1979 [Syracuse 144, Sienna 92].)
16) A – NYU (The Orange lost 59-122 to the Violets on Dec. 15, 1961.)
17) B – 4 (Danforth led the Orange to the NCAA Tournament from 1973-76.)
18) C – 51 (The Orange beat Le Moyne 85-51 on Nov. 16, 2008 and Colgate 86-51 on Dec. 1, 2008.)
19) B – 6 games (Syracuse won every meeting from Feb. 10, 1996 through Feb. 27, 2000.)
20) B – No (Syracuse has an all-time record of 50-32 in the NCAA Tournament for a .610 winning percentage.)
21) C – 3 (1983-84, 1990-91, and 1999-00)
22) B – 10 (The last time the Orange finished in the top 10 was a No. 7 ranking following the 1990-91 season.)

# Regular Season — Answer Key
## Orangeology Trivia Challenge

23) D – Dwayne Washington (He won the award for the 1983-84 season. Other SU players to win the award are Derrick Coleman [1986-87], Lawrence Moten [1991-92], Carmelo Anthony [2002-03], and Jonny Flynn [2007-08].)

24) C – 65 (Navy set this record against SU in the second half of an NCAA Tournament game on March 16, 1986 [SU 85, Navy 97].)

25) A – Lewis Andreas (He led SU to 358 wins during his 25 seasons as head coach.)

26) A – Yes (Syracuse lost 49-63 to Connecticut on Feb. 11, 2009.)

27) B – 583 (Jonny Flynn led the team with 129 and Eric Devendorf was second with 107.)

28) C – 34 (Frank Reddout recorded 34 rebounds against Temple on Feb. 9, 1952 [Syracuse 64, Temple 47].)

29) D – 17 (Paul Harris led the Orange with 10 points in the sixth overtime [SU 127, UConn 117].)

30) D – 39 (Syracuse had a winning record every season between the 1971-72 season and 2008-09 season.)

31) A Connecticut (The Orange beat the Huskies 82-76 in their first-ever NCAA Tournament game on March 12, 1957.)

32) B – 3 (Derrick Coleman [1989-90], Billy Owens [1990-91] and Hakim Warrick [2004-05])

# Regular Season — Answer Key
## Orangeology Trivia Challenge

33) C – 15 (The Orange accomplished this feat twice: against West Virginia on Jan. 16, 1997 and East Tennessee State on Dec. 15, 2008.)
34) B – 12 (1946, 1950, 1964, 1967, 1971, 1972, 1981, 1982, 1997, 2002, 2007, and 2008)
35) A – 27 (The Orange lost by 27 points to the Hoyas on Feb. 1, 1943 [Syracuse 38, Georgetown 65] and March 3, 1985 [Syracuse 63, Georgetown 90].)
36) C – Dave Bing (He scored in double figures in 66 consecutive games from 1963-66.)
37) D – Eric Devendorf (He made 97 of 122 free-throw attempts for a .795 percentage made.)
38) B – 7 (Jim Lee [1975], Sherman Douglas [1987], Derrick Coleman [1987], Todd Burgan [1996], John Wallace [1996], Carmelo Anthony [2003], and Gerry McNamara [2003])
39) A – Yes (Jason Hart recorded 101 steals in 1998-99 and James Thues recorded 101 in 2001-02.)
40) A – 1945-46 (Syracuse finished the season 23-4.)
41) D – Pittsburgh (SU is 61-36 all-time against Pittsburgh for a .629 winning percentage.)
42) C – Stephen F. Austin (Syracuse beat the 14th seeded Lumberjacks 59-44.)
43) B – Derrick Coleman (He played in 143 career games with Syracuse from the 1986-87 season through the 1989-90 season.)

# Regular Season — Answer Key
## Orangeology Trivia Challenge

44) A – 2 (The Orange won back-to-back regular-season titles in 1985-86 and 1986-87 and then again in 1989-90 and 1990-91.)

45) B – No (Dave Bing came the closest in 1966 when he was the nation's fifth leading scorer with an average of 28.4 points per game.)

46) C – Gene Waldron (He scored 40 points against Iona on Dec. 4, 1983 [Syracuse 109, Iona 92].)

47) C – 5 (Jonny Flynn [17.4], Eric Devendorf [15.7], Paul Harris [12.0], Andy Rautins [10.5], and Arinze Onuaku [10.3])

48) A – Colgate (The Orange has an all-time record of 116-45 against the Raiders.)

49) A – 1979-80 (Syracuse finished 5-1 in conference play and won the Big East title in the inaugural season.)

50) D – Oklahoma State (The Orange played the Cowboys in 2004 [Syracuse 60, OSU 74] and again in 2006 [Syracuse 68, OSU 72].)

Note: All answers valid as of the end of the 2008-09 season, unless otherwise indicated in the question itself.

**Conference Tournament** / 3-Point Questions

## Orangeology Trivia Challenge

1) How many times has Syracuse appeared in the Big East Tournament Championship game?

Answers begin on page 56

   A) 9
   B) 12
   C) 14
   D) 16

2) What is the SU record for most free throws made in a single game?

   A) 16
   B) 18
   C) 21
   D) 23

3) Which season did the Orange first record 30 wins?

   A) 1986-87
   B) 1989-90
   C) 1994-95
   D) 1999-00

4) Did any Orange player have greater than fifty steals in 2008-09?

   A) Yes
   B) No

## Conference Tournament — 3-Point Questions
### Orangeology Trivia Challenge

5) What are the most consecutive games the Orange has won at Madison Square Garden?

    A) 2
    B) 4
    C) 6
    D) 9

6) What is SU's record for most consecutive winning seasons?

    A) 21
    B) 28
    C) 34
    D) 39

7) What was the name of the first official home of Syracuse basketball?

    A) Archbold Gym
    B) Syracuse Hill
    C) Scott Arena
    D) Orange Stadium

8) In the SU Alma Mater, where does the vale of Onondaga meet?

    A) Eyes of Victory
    B) Eastern Sky
    C) Hilltop High
    D) Western Sky

**Conference Tournament** / 3-Point Questions

*Orangeology Trivia Challenge*

9) When was the last time SU lost a home opener?

    A) 1997-98
    B) 1999-00
    C) 2003-04
    D) 2005-06

10) Was Derrick Coleman named to an All-American team every season he played for Syracuse?

    A) Yes
    B) No

11) Who holds Syracuse's record for most steals in a career?

    A) Eddie Moss
    B) Adrian Autry
    C) Jason Hart
    D) Billy Owens

12) Who was the last freshman to lead Syracuse in scoring for a single season?

    A) Carmelo Anthony
    B) Lawrence Moten
    C) Rafael Addison
    D) Donte Greene

## Conference Tournament — 3-Point Questions
### *Orangeology Trivia Challenge*

13) Who coached the Orange immediately prior to Jim Boeheim?

   A) Edmund Dollard
   B) Fred Lewis
   C) Roy Danforth
   D) Marc Guley

14) Has Syracuse ever had a player drafted No. 1 overall in the NBA Draft?

   A) Yes
   B) No

15) What is SU's largest-ever margin of victory over Georgetown?

   A) 32
   B) 35
   C) 38
   D) 41

16) Who was SU's only player listed as under 6'0" on the 2008-09 roster?

   A) Jonny Flynn
   B) Brandon Reese
   C) Jake Presutti
   D) Scoop Jardine

**Conference Tournament** / 3-Point Questions

*Orangeology Trivia Challenge*

17) SU's Jim Boeheim ranks among the top five Division I coaches with the most career wins.

   A) True
   B) False

18) Who was the leading scorer for the Orange in the 1996 NCAA Tournament Championship game?

   A) Todd Burgan
   B) Lazarus Sims
   C) John Wallace
   D) Otis Hill

19) What is the name of Syracuse's basketball court?

   A) Jim Boeheim Court
   B) Carrier Court
   C) Bing Court
   D) Orange Court

20) Who was Syracuse's first-ever official basketball coach?

   A) Edmund Dollard
   B) Lewis Andreas
   C) Marc Guley
   D) John A.R. Scott

## Conference Tournament — 3-Point Questions
### Orangeology Trivia Challenge

21) Against which team was the Orange's last regular-season Big East loss in 2008-09?

   A) Rutgers
   B) St John's
   C) Villanova
   D) Providence

22) In 2008-09, each of Syracuse's single-game leading scorers had 15 or more points.

   A) True
   B) False

23) How many times has SU made the NCAA Tournament in the program's history?

   A) 28
   B) 32
   C) 35
   D) 42

24) What is SU's record for fewest points scored in a game?

   A) 3
   B) 8
   C) 11
   D) 14

## Conference Tournament — 3-Point Questions
### Orangeology Trivia Challenge

25) Which decade did SU rank in the top five for best winning percentage amongst Division I teams?

   A) 1930s
   B) 1950s
   C) 1980s
   D) 1990s

26) Since its inception, how many times has Syracuse appeared in the NCAA Tournament Championship game?

   A) 2
   B) 3
   C) 4
   D) 5

27) How many times has Syracuse been Big East Regular Season Champions?

   A) 5
   B) 7
   C) 9
   D) 10

28) Who was the first-ever African-American to play for Syracuse?

   A) Vinnie Cohen
   B) Ronnie Kilpatrick
   C) Manny Breland
   D) Wilmeth Sidat-Singh

## Conference Tournament — 3-Point Questions
### Orangeology Trivia Challenge

29) What were the most consecutive wins by Syracuse in the 2008-09 season?

   A) 5
   B) 7
   C) 9
   D) 10

30) Has any Syracuse player ever worn jersey number 00?

   A) Yes
   B) No

31) Who scored Syracuse's first points in the 2009 NCAA Tournament?

   A) Paul Harris
   B) Eric Devendorf
   C) Rick Jackson
   D) Arinze Onuaku

32) What is the Orange's record for most points scored in one half?

   A) 69
   B) 71
   C) 75
   D) 80

## Conference Tournament / 3-Point Questions
### Orangeology Trivia Challenge

33) When was the only time a No. 1-ranked Syracuse team lost to an unranked opponent?

   A) 1979
   B) 1988
   C) 1990
   D) 2003

34) Who was the last Syracuse player to average 20 or more points per game for two or more consecutive seasons?

   A) Billy Owens
   B) John Wallace
   C) Lawrence Moten
   D) Greg Kohls

35) What is Syracuse's record for most points allowed in a regulation game at the Carrier Dome?

   A) 99
   B) 103
   C) 112
   D) 119

36) How many Syracuse head coaches lasted one season or less?

   A) 0
   B) 1
   C) 2
   D) 4

## Conference Tournament — 3-Point Questions
### Orangeology Trivia Challenge

37) Carmelo Anthony recorded a double-double in the 2003 NCAA Tournament Championship game.

   A) True
   B) False

38) Which team gave SU its first-ever home loss at the Carrier Dome?

   A) Penn State
   B) Rutgers
   C) Maryland
   D) Detroit

39) Which Big East school has the highest winning percentage against the Orange?

   A) Cincinnati
   B) Villanova
   C) Providence
   D) Louisville

40) What is Syracuse's record for most losses in one season at the Carrier Dome?

   A) 5
   B) 7
   C) 8
   D) 10

# Conference Tournament — 3-Point Questions
## Orangeology Trivia Challenge

41) What is SU's record for most consecutive NCAA Tournament wins?

   A) 4
   B) 6
   C) 8
   D) 10

42) How many times has an SU player won the Dave Gavitt Trophy, given to the Big East Tournament MVP?

   A) 2
   B) 4
   C) 6
   D) 8

43) Who holds the SU record for best field-goal percentage in a single season?

   A) Stephen Thompson
   B) Bill Smith
   C) Etan Thomas
   D) Roosevelt Bouie

44) Has any Syracuse player ever been named NBA Rookie of the Year?

   A) Yes
   B) No

## Conference Tournament — 3-Point Questions
## Orangeology Trivia Challenge

45) In how many games was SU's Jonny Flynn perfect from the line in the 2008-09 season?

   A) 0
   B) 2
   C) 4
   D) 7

46) Was Syracuse ranked in the Preseason AP Poll prior to the 2002-03 season?

   A) Yes
   B) No

47) What was the nickname of the student section at Manley Field House?

   A) Zoo
   B) Pulpinators
   C) Orange Crazies
   D) 'Cuse Crazies

48) How many Orange are in the Naismith Memorial Basketball Hall of Fame as players?

   A) 0
   B) 1
   C) 2
   D) 4

## Conference Tournament — 3-Point Questions
### Orangeology Trivia Challenge

49) In the 2008-09 season, how many times did the Orange win a game after trailing at halftime?

    A) 3
    B) 5
    C) 7
    D) 9

50) What is Syracuse's record for most consecutive Big East wins?

    A) 9
    B) 12
    C) 15
    D) 18

## Conference Tournament

## Cool Fact

### Orangeology Trivia Challenge

The Orange had a great start to the 1907-08 season. The team was 8-0 and outscoring opponents by an average of 12.9 points per game. The season was setting up to be the first undefeated season in Syracuse history. The ninth game of the season was an away game at Wesleyan. The game was a very physical matchup and the officiating seemed to be lopsided in favor of Wesleyan. With the Orange leading 22-16 in the second half, team captain and future Syracuse head coach Edmund Dollard called a timeout. Dollard used the timeout to protest the officiating. His protest greatly backfired when the official proclaimed that SU had withdrawn from the game and therefore forfeited to Wesleyan. This game marks the only forfeit in Syracuse history. The disappointment continued into the next two games as the team was outscored by an average 12.5 points in those games. Syracuse won the last two and finished the season 10-3.

## Conference Tournament — Answer Key
### *Orangeology Trivia Challenge*

1) D – 16 (1981, 1984, 1986-90, 1992, 1993, 1996, 1998, 1999, 2001, 2005, 2006, and 2009)
2) B – 18 (Allen Griffin made 18 free throws against St. John's on March 4, 2001 and Hakim Warrick made 18 against Connecticut on Nov. 30, 2003.)
3) A – 1986-87 (Syracuse finished the season 31-7.)
4) A – Yes (Jonny Flynn led the team with 54 steals. Andy Rautins is the only other player to surpass 50 steals for the season with 52.)
5) C – 6 (SU won all four games played at MSG in the 1987-88 season and the first two of the 1988-89 season.)
6) D – 39 (SU has had a winning season every year since 1971.)
7) A – Archbold Gym (The Orange played here from 1908-47 and again from 1952-55.)
8) B – Eastern Sky ("Where the vale of Onondaga meets the eastern sky....")
9) D – 2005-06 (The Orange lost 69-75 to Bucknell in the home opener.)
10) A – Yes (He was named honorable mention by The Sporting News in 1987 and 1988. He was named to various lists in 1989 and was consensus All-American in 1990.)
11) C – Jason Hart (He recorded 329 steals over 132 games from 1996-00.)

## Conference Tournament — Answer Key
### Orangeology Trivia Challenge

12) D – Donte Greene (He led the team with 620 points in the 2007-08 season. The only other freshman to lead the team in scoring was Carmelo Anthony with 778 points in the 2002-03 season.)
13) C – Roy Danforth (Boeheim was an assistant under Danforth before taking the head coaching job in 1976.)
14) A – Yes (Derrick Coleman was drafted No. 1 overall by the New Jersey Nets in the 1990 NBA Draft.)
15) A – 32 (The Orange beat the Hoyas 40-18 on Feb. 15, 1930.)
16) B – Brandon Reese (He was listed as 5'11", playing in 16 games as a freshman for SU in 2008-09.)
17) B – False (Boeheim ranks eighth overall in the category of most all-time coaching victories – he ranks third amongst current active coaches.)
18) C – John Wallace (He led the team with 29 points. The only other player in double figures was Todd Burgan with 19.)
19) A – Jim Boeheim Court (The 225 piece court is assembled in the west end zone for basketball games.)
20) D – John A.R. Scott (He coached Syracuse from 1903-11 and led the Orange to a record of 64-54 for a .542 winning percentage.)
21) C – Villanova (The Orange lost 86-89 to the Wildcats on Feb. 22, 2009.)

## Conference Tournament — Answer Key

### Orangeology Trivia Challenge

22) B – False (Rick Jackson was the leading scorer with 14 points against Canisius and Andy Rautins was the leading scorer with 14 points against South Florida.)
23) B – 32 (The last time the Orange appeared in the NCAA Tournament was in 2009.)
24) A – 3 (SU lost 3-49 to Colgate on Feb. 14, 1903.)
25) A – 1930s (SU ranked fifth amongst Division I teams with a record of 143-37 for a .794 winning percentage.)
26) B – 3 (1987, 1996, and 2003)
27) B – 7 (1979-80, 1985-86, 1986-87, 1989-90, 1990-91, 1999-00, and 2002-03)
28) D – Wilmeth Sidat-Singh (He played for the Orange from the 1936-37 season through the 1938-39 season. He was the leading scorer his senior year.)
29) C – 9 (Syracuse started out the season 9-0.)
30) A – Yes (Rick Jackson is the only player to wear the jersey number. He is currently a junior on the 2009-10 roster.)
31) D – Arinze Onuaku (He made a layup 38 seconds into the game to give SU a two-point lead against Stephen F. Austin.)
32) C – 75 (The Orange scored 75 points in the second half against Sienna on Jan. 17, 1979 [Syracuse 144, Siena 92].)

## Conference Tournament
### Orangeology Trivia Challenge
**Answer Key**

33) C – 1990 (Syracuse lost 74-93 to an unranked Villanova.)
34) D – Greg Kohls (He averaged 22.1 points per game in 1970-71 and 26.7 points per game in 1971-72. Bill Smith [two seasons] and Dave Bing [three seasons] are the only other players to accomplish this feat.)
35) B – 103 (SU lost 91-103 to Notre Dame on Jan. 30, 2007.)
36) A – 0 (Fred Lewis had the shortest tenure of Orange head coaches, six seasons from the 1962-63 season until the 1967-68 season.)
37) A – True (Anthony led the team with 20 points and 10 rebounds.)
38) C – Maryland (The Orange lost 73-83 to the Terrapins in the third home game in the Carrier Dome.)
39) D – Louisville (SU has an all-time record of 4-10 against the Cardinals for a .286 winning percentage.)
40) B – 7 (SU finished 9-7 at home in 1996-97 and again in 1998-99.)
41) C – 8 (Syracuse won all six games of the 2003 NCAA Tournament and two games in 2004.)
42) C – 6 (Leo Rautins [1981], Dwayne Washington [1986], Sherman Douglas [1988], Hakim Warrick [2005], Gerry McNamara [2006], and Jonny Flynn [2009])
43) D – Roosevelt Bouie (He made 189 of 289 attempts in the 1979-80 season for a .654 percentage.)

*Syracuse Orange Basketball*

## Conference Tournament — Answer Key
### Orangeology Trivia Challenge

44) A – Yes (Dave Bing won the award in 1966-67 and Derrick Coleman won in 1990-91.)
45) D – 7 (He combined for a perfect 33-33 in these games, which includes 16-16 in the six overtime win against Connecticut.)
46) B – No (Syracuse was unranked to start the season and finished the season ranked 13th overall before going on to win their first NCAA Tournament title.)
47) A – Zoo (This was due to the rowdiness and excessive noise the section would make.)
48) C – 2 (Vic Hanson was enshrined in 1960 and Dave Bing was enshrined in 1990.)
49) C – 7 (Seven of Syracuse's 28 wins came after trailing at halftime.)
50) B – 12 (The Orange won the last five conference games of the 2003-04 season and the first seven of the 2004-05 season.)

Note: All answers valid as of the end of the 2008-09 season, unless otherwise indicated in the question itself.

# Championship Game — 4-Point Questions
## Orangeology Trivia Challenge

1) Does Syracuse have a winning record against every member of the ACC?

    A) Yes
    B) No

Answers begin on page 75

2) Which game set Syracuse's attendance record at the Carrier Dome?

    A) Connecticut 2004
    B) Georgetown 1991
    C) Notre Dame 2005
    D) Villanova 2006

3) How many times has Syracuse beaten a team ranked No. 1 in the AP Poll?

    A) 2
    B) 3
    C) 5
    D) 7

4) What is SU's all-time worst seed in the NCAA Tournament?

    A) 7 seed
    B) 8 seed
    C) 11 seed
    D) 12 seed

# Championship Game / 4-Point Questions
## Orangeology Trivia Challenge

5) Who was Syracuse's first-ever Big East opponent?

   A) Seton Hall
   B) Providence
   C) St. John's
   D) Georgetown

6) What is SU's largest-ever margin of victory over Connecticut?

   A) 31 points
   B) 34 points
   C) 37 points
   D) 40 points

7) Excluding St. John's, who is the last intrastate opponent to beat the Orange?

   A) Fordham
   B) Niagara
   C) St. Bonaventure
   D) Canisius

8) Who holds the Orange's record for most points scored in a freshman season?

   A) Carmelo Anthony
   B) Billy Owens
   C) Jack Kiley
   D) Dave Bing

## Championship Game — 4-Point Questions
### Orangeology Trivia Challenge

9) Did Syracuse attempt more free throws than its opponents in the 2008-09 season?

    A) Yes
    B) No

10) What is the Orange's record for most team rebounds in a single game?

    A) 71
    B) 76
    C) 84
    D) 87

11) Who holds SU's record for most points scored in an NCAA Tournament game?

    A) Derrick Coleman
    B) Carmelo Anthony
    C) Jonny Flynn
    D) Gerry McNamara

12) When did the Orange first travel out of state for a basketball game?

    A) 1903
    B) 1905
    C) 1907
    D) 1910

## Championship Game — 4-Point Questions
### Orangeology Trivia Challenge

13) In which category did Syracuse lead the nation in 1979?

    A) Field-Goal Percentage
    B) Blocks
    C) Rebounds
    D) Scoring Margin

14) How many times has Syracuse been beaten while ranked No. 1 in the AP Poll?

    A) 1
    B) 3
    C) 5
    D) 7

15) How many times in school history has Syracuse won 30 or more games in a season?

    A) 1
    B) 3
    C) 5
    D) 6

16) How many games did it take Jim Boeheim to get to 500 career victories?

    A) 598
    B) 621
    C) 647
    D) 670

## Championship Game — 4-Point Questions
### Orangeology Trivia Challenge

17) In 2008-09, did any Syracuse player have 10 or more turnovers in a single game?

   A) Yes
   B) No

18) All time, how many total weeks has Syracuse held the No. 1 ranking in the AP Poll?

   A) 7
   B) 12
   C) 19
   D) 24

19) When was the most recent season Syracuse scored fewer than 2,500 points as a team?

   A) 1994-95
   B) 1999-00
   C) 2003-04
   D) 2006-07

20) What is the Orange's record for most consecutive NCAA Tournament losses?

   A) 2
   B) 3
   C) 5
   D) 6

## Championship Game / 4-Point Questions
## Orangeology Trivia Challenge

21) How many losing seasons did Jim Boeheim's predecessor, Roy Danforth, have at SU?

    A) 0
    B) 1
    C) 3
    D) 5

22) Since 1970, how many seasons has Syracuse led the nation in average attendance per game?

    A) 8
    B) 10
    C) 12
    D) 14

23) Syracuse is the only team Jim Boeheim has ever coached.

    A) True
    B) False

24) Which is the only Pac-10 school with an all-time winning record against Syracuse?

    A) UCLA
    B) Arizona
    C) Washington
    D) Arizona State

## Championship Game / 4-Point Questions
### Orangeology Trivia Challenge

25) When was SU's team record for most points scored in a season set?

   A) 1975-76
   B) 1979-80
   C) 1988-89
   D) 1993-94

26) Has Syracuse surpassed the all-time 2,000-win mark?

   A) Yes
   B) No

27) How many times has Syracuse been a No. 1 seed in the NCAA Tournament?

   A) 1
   B) 2
   C) 3
   D) 4

28) How many losing seasons did Syracuse have without a head coach?

   A) 0
   B) 1
   C) 2
   D) 3

## Championship Game — 4-Point Questions
### Orangeology Trivia Challenge

29) Which decade did SU have its lowest winning percentage?

   A) 1900s
   B) 1930s
   C) 1950s
   D) 1980s

30) When was the most recent season Syracuse had a losing record in the Big East?

   A) 2001-02
   B) 2004-05
   C) 2005-06
   D) 2007-08

31) How many Orange players have scored 1,000 or more career points?

   A) 38
   B) 41
   C) 47
   D) 51

32) Against which major conference does Syracuse have the best all-time record?

   A) Pac-10
   B) Big 12
   C) SEC
   D) Big Ten

## Championship Game — 4-Point Questions
### Orangeology Trivia Challenge

33) What is SU's record for largest-ever margin of victory in an NCAA Tournament game?

   A) 41 points
   B) 46 points
   C) 49 points
   D) 55 points

34) Which Orange player had the highest three-point percentage in 2008-09 (minimum 25 attempts)?

   A) Andy Rautins
   B) Paul Harris
   C) Jake Presutti
   D) Eric Devendorf

35) When was the most recent season the Orange made over 50% of their shots from the field?

   A) 1988-89
   B) 1992-93
   C) 1999-00
   D) 2002-03

36) Has Syracuse ever had more than one player selected in the first round of the NBA Draft in the same year?

   A) Yes
   B) No

## Championship Game — 4-Point Questions
### Orangeology Trivia Challenge

37) Who was the most recent player to lead Syracuse in scoring for three seasons?

   A) Sherman Douglas
   B) Vinnie Cohen
   C) John Wallace
   D) Lawrence Moten

38) Syracuse's National Championship team also won the Big East regular season and conference tournament.

   A) True
   B) False

39) What is SU's record for most consecutive 20-win seasons?

   A) 11
   B) 14
   C) 17
   D) 21

40) What was Syracuse's winning percentage at Manley Field House?

   A) .741
   B) .788
   C) .809
   D) .864

# Championship Game — 4-Point Questions
## Orangeology Trivia Challenge

41) How many Orange averaged 20 or more minutes of playing time per game in the 2008-09 season?

   A) 4
   B) 6
   C) 8
   D) 9

42) Who was the most recent Orange named CoSIDA First Team Academic All-American?

   A) Dennis DuVal
   B) Hal Cohen
   C) Dan Schayes
   D) Craig Forth

43) Which of the following players did not score over 2,000 career points while at Syracuse?

   A) Gerry McNamara
   B) Dave Bing
   C) Derrick Coleman
   D) Hakim Warrick

44) What is SU's longest-ever winning streak in the Carrier Dome?

   A) 19 games
   B) 21 games
   C) 24 games
   D) 28 games

## Championship Game / 4-Point Questions
### Orangeology Trivia Challenge

45) Who is the only Syracuse player to be awarded Big East Defensive Player of the Year?

   A) Gene Waldron
   B) Hakim Warrick
   C) Gerry McNamara
   D) Etan Thomas

46) Where did Syracuse head coach Jim Boeheim play college basketball?

   A) Syracuse
   B) St. John's
   C) North Carolina
   D) Michigan State

47) Does Syracuse have a losing record against any of the five major conferences (Big Ten, Big 12, Pac-10, ACC, or SEC)?

   A) Yes
   B) No

48) Which school was Syracuse's first opponent at Madison Square Garden?

   A) Brown
   B) Colgate
   C) Manhattan
   D) Rutgers

## Championship Game — 4-Point Questions
### Orangeology Trivia Challenge

49) How many points did SU score in the first half of the 2003 NCAA Tournament Championship game?

    A) 47
    B) 49
    C) 51
    D) 53

50) Which team broke Syracuse's 57-game home-court winning streak?

    A) Louisville
    B) Georgetown
    C) Maryland
    D) Cincinnati

## Championship Game

## Cool Fact

*Orangeology Trivia Challenge*

Dave Bing is one of the best players to ever play for the Orange. He led the team in scoring for three years and was a First Team Consensus All-American his senior year. Later he was drafted by the Detroit Pistons. Midway through his twelve year NBA career during a preseason game in 1971-72 he was hit in the face. A doctor later informed him that as a result his retina had detached. This would be a terrible fate for any athlete, but it was especially so for Bing. This is because his other eye was pierced by a nail when he was five years old. Prior to the incident in 1971, Bing had been playing with only one good eye and blurred vision in the other. He returned to average 22.6 points per game and scored 8,967 points the seven seasons following the second eye injury. We can only imagine what Bing might have done if he had ever played with two good eyes.

## Championship Game — Answer Key
### Orangeology Trivia Challenge

1) B – No (Clemson [2-2], Georgia Tech [1-2], Maryland [3-5], and North Carolina 2-4].)
2) D – Villanova 2006 (This game on March 5, 2006 set an NCAA on-campus attendance record with 33,633 [Syracuse 82, Villanova 92].)
3) B – 3 (Eleventh ranked Syracuse beat No. 1 Georgetown 65-63 on Jan. 28, 1985, 17th ranked Syracuse beat No. 1 UConn 59-42 on Feb. 1, 1999, and unranked Syracuse beat No. 1 UConn 86-84 on March 9, 2006.)
4) B – 8 seed (The Orange lost 61-69 to 7 seed Oklahoma State in the first round of the 1999 NCAA Tournament.)
5) A – Seton Hall (The Orange beat the Pirates 99-76 on Jan. 5, 1980.)
6) D – 40 points (The Orange beat the Huskies 101-61 on Nov. 30, 1977.)
7) – St. Bonaventure (The Orange lost 71-74 to the Bonnies on Jan. 26, 1981.)
8) A – Carmelo Anthony (He scored 778 points his freshman season, 2002-03.)
9) A – Yes (SU attempted 884 free throws as a team while their opponents attempted 644.)
10) C – 84 (The Orange pulled down 84 team rebounds against Massachusetts on Jan. 29, 1966 [Syracuse 114, Massachusetts 72].)
11) D – Gerry McNamara (He scored 43 points against BYU in the first round of the 2004 tournament.)

## Championship Game — Answer Key
### Orangeology Trivia Challenge

12) A – 1903 (The Orange traveled to Allegheny, Pa. to play the Allegheny Gators [Syracuse 11, Allegheny 25].)
13) D – Scoring Margin (SU averaged 88.7 points per game, while allowing only 71.5 points per game.)
14) B – 3 (SU was ranked No. 1 when they fell 93-96 to 3rd ranked North Carolina on Nov. 21, 1987, 69-80 to 17th ranked Arizona on Nov. 30, 1987, and 74-93 to unranked Villanova on Jan. 6, 1990.)
15) B – 3 (Syracuse finished 31-7 in the 1986-87, 30-8 in the 1988-89, and 30-5 in the 2002-03 season.)
16) D – 670 (Boeheim received his 500th win against Providence on Feb. 24, 1997.)
17) B – No (The most turnovers by a single player in a game was 7. Flynn had 7 turnovers in three different games and Devendorf had 7 in two different games.)
18) A – 7 (One week in the 1987-88 season and six weeks in the 1989-90 season)
19) C – 2003-04 (The Orange scored 2,265 points as a team for the season.)
20) B – 3 (SU lost to Alabama in the Sweet 16 of 2004 and the first round of the 2005 and 2006 Tournaments.)
21) B – 1 (Danforth's only losing season with SU was his first season. He led the Orange to a record of 127-43 [.747] his last six seasons and an overall record of 148-71 [.676] from 1968-76.)
22) C – 12 (1984-85 through the 1994-95 seasons and the 2004-05 season)

## Championship Game — Answer Key
### Orangeology Trivia Challenge

23) A – True (Boeheim was a graduate assistant at SU from 1969-71 and a full-time assistant from 1972-76 before taking the head coach position for the 1976-77 season.)
24) D – Arizona State (SU is 0-1 all-time against ASU.)
25) C – 1988-89 (The Orange scored 3,410 points as a team over 38 games for an average of 89.7 PPG.)
26) B – No (Syracuse has an all-time record of 1,753-806 for a .685 winning percentage.)
27) A – 1 (SU was the number one seed in the East Region in the 1980 NCAA Tournament. Seeding did not begin until the 1979 tournament.)
28) B – 0 (Syracuse finished 2-2 in 1900-01, 3-3 in 1901-02, and 1-8 in 1902-03 before John A. R. Scott was named head coach for the 1903-04 season.)
29) C – 1950s (The Orange finished the decade with a 119-122 overall record for a .494 winning percentage.)
30) C – 2005-06 (SU finished 7-9 in conference play and tied for ninth place.)
31) D – 51 (Jonny Flynn and Paul Harris were the most recent players to surpass the 1,000 career point mark in the 2008-09 season.)
32) A – Pac-10 (SU is 7-4 all-time against the Pac-10 for a .636 winning percentage.)
33) C – 49 points (SU beat Brown 101-52 in the first round of the 1986 NCAA Tournament.)
34) D – Eric Devendorf (He shot 82-210 from three-point range for a .390 percentage.)

## Championship Game — Answer Key
### Orangeology Trivia Challenge

35) A – 1988-89 (The Orange shot 1,334-2,456 for a field-goal percentage of .543.)

36) A – Yes (Billy Owens was selected no. 3 overall by Sacramento and LeRon Ellis was selected no 22 overall by the LA Clippers in the 1991 NBA Draft.)

37) D – Lawrence Moten (He led the team in scoring from 1992-93 to the 1994-95 season. The only other SU players to lead the team for 3 seasons are Billy Gabor, Jack Kiley, Vinnie Cohen, Dave Bing, and Sherman Douglas.)

38) B – False (The 2002-03 team tied with Pittsburgh as co-champions of the Big East West and Pittsburgh won the conference tournament.)

39) B – 14 (The Orange won 20 or more games from 1982-83 to 1995-96.)

40) D – .864 (SU has an all-time record of 190-30 at Manley Field House.)

41) B – 6 (Jonny Flynn [37.3], Eric Devendorf [33.9], Paul Harris [30.5], Andy Rautins [28.6], Arinze Onuaku [26.8], and Rick Jackson [22.1])

42) C – Dan Schayes (He was named First-Team Academic All-American in 1981, and remains the only Orange to receive this honor.)

43) B – Dave Bing (Bing had 1,883 career points. Six Orange have surpassed 2,000 points: Lawrence Moten [2,334], Derrick Coleman [2,143], John Wallace [2,119], Gerry McNamara [2,099], Hakim Warrick [2,073], and Sherman Douglas [2,060].)

## Championship Game
## Answer Key
### Orangeology Trivia Challenge

44) C – 24 games (The Orange won the last 12 home games of 1993-94 and the first 12 of the 1994-95 season.)

45) D – Etan Thomas (He won the award in 1999 and again in 2000.)

46) A – Syracuse (Boeheim played for SU from 1962-63 to 1965-66.)

47) B – No (Syracuse's records [including winning percentage] against the major conferences are: Big Ten 80-66 [.548], ACC 72-47 [.605], Pac-10 7-4 [.636], SEC 20-16 [.556], and Big 12 18-11 [.621].)

48) C – Manhattan (The Orange beat the Jaspers 42-31 on Feb. 1, 1939 in the first of 65 seasons of Orange basketball games played at Madison Square Garden.)

49) D – 53 (This set a record for most points scored in the first half of a championship game.)

50) B – Georgetown (SU lost 50-52 to the Hoyas on Feb. 12, 1980, in the last home game in Manley Field House.)

Note: All answers valid as of the end of the 2008-09 season, unless otherwise indicated in the question itself.

# Overtime Bonus — 4-Point Questions
## Orangeology Trivia Challenge

Answers begin on page 83

1) For which team did Jim Boeheim play professional basketball?

   A) New York Knicks
   B) New Jersey Nets
   C) Scranton Miners
   D) Rochester Warriors

2) How many times has Syracuse opened the season ranked No. 1 in the first AP Poll?

   A) 0
   B) 1
   C) 2
   D) 3

3) When was the first time the Orange surpassed 3,000 points as a team in a single season?

   A) 1971-72
   B) 1975-76
   C) 1980-81
   D) 1986-87

4) Did Coach Boeheim win his first-ever game as head coach of Syracuse?

   A) Yes
   B) No

*Syracuse Orange Basketball*

# Overtime Bonus — 4-Point Questions
## Orangeology Trivia Challenge

5) When was the first-ever season Syracuse scored 100 points in a regulation game?

    A) 1945-46
    B) 1952-53
    C) 1960-61
    D) 1968-69

6) How many foreign born players were on Syracuse's 2008-09 roster?

    A) 0
    B) 1
    C) 2
    D) 3

7) Which player holds Syracuse's record for most points scored in an NCAA Championship game?

    A) Carmelo Anthony
    B) Howard Triche
    C) Derrick Coleman
    D) John Wallace

8) Since 1957, how many Syracuse players have been drafted in the first round of the NBA Draft?

    A) 12
    B) 16
    C) 19
    D) 22

# Overtime Bonus / 4-Point Questions
## Orangeology Trivia Challenge

9) What were Syracuse's originally chosen school colors?

　　A)　Yellow and Green
　　B)　Orange and Black
　　C)　Navy Blue and Scarlet
　　D)　Rose Pink and Pea Green

10) Did Syracuse trail at halftime in the 2003 NCAA Championship game?

　　A)　Yes
　　B)　No

## Overtime Bonus — Answer Key
### Orangeology Trivia Challenge

1) C – Scranton Miners (He played 136 games for Scranton from 1966-72.)
2) B – 1 (Syracuse opened the 1987-88 season ranked number one.)
3) D – 1986-87 (The Orange scored 3,145 points and finished the season 31-7.)
4) A – Yes (Boeheim led the Orange to a 75-48 win against Harvard on Nov. 26, 1976.)
5) A – 1945-46 (The Orange beat the Oswego Teachers 106-25 on Dec. 8, 1945.)
6) C – 2 (Kristof Ongenaet [Belgium] and Kris Joseph [Canada])
7) D – John Wallace (He scored 29 points in the 1996 NCAA Championship game.)
8) B – 16 (Jonny Flynn was the most recent Orange to be drafted in the first round [6th overall to Minnesota in 2009].)
9) D – Rose Pink and Pea Green (These were the first official colors adopted in 1872. The colors were changed to rose tint and azure the following year.)
10) B – No (The Orange led the Jayhawks 53-42 at halftime.)

Note: All answers valid as of the end of the 2008-09 season, unless otherwise indicated in the question itself.

# Player / Team Score Sheet

Name: _____

| Preseason | | Regular Season | | Conference Tournament | | Championship Game | | Overtime Bonus | |
|---|---|---|---|---|---|---|---|---|---|
| 1 | 26 | 1 | 26 | 1 | 26 | 1 | 26 | 1 | |
| 2 | 27 | 2 | 27 | 2 | 27 | 2 | 27 | 2 | |
| 3 | 28 | 3 | 28 | 3 | 28 | 3 | 28 | 3 | |
| 4 | 29 | 4 | 29 | 4 | 29 | 4 | 29 | 4 | |
| 5 | 30 | 5 | 30 | 5 | 30 | 5 | 30 | 5 | |
| 6 | 31 | 6 | 31 | 6 | 31 | 6 | 31 | 6 | |
| 7 | 32 | 7 | 32 | 7 | 32 | 7 | 32 | 7 | |
| 8 | 33 | 8 | 33 | 8 | 33 | 8 | 33 | 8 | |
| 9 | 34 | 9 | 34 | 9 | 34 | 9 | 34 | 9 | |
| 10 | 35 | 10 | 35 | 10 | 35 | 10 | 35 | 10 | |
| 11 | 36 | 11 | 36 | 11 | 36 | 11 | 36 | | |
| 12 | 37 | 12 | 37 | 12 | 37 | 12 | 37 | | |
| 13 | 38 | 13 | 38 | 13 | 38 | 13 | 38 | | |
| 14 | 39 | 14 | 39 | 14 | 39 | 14 | 39 | | |
| 15 | 40 | 15 | 40 | 15 | 40 | 15 | 40 | | |
| 16 | 41 | 16 | 41 | 16 | 41 | 16 | 41 | | |
| 17 | 42 | 17 | 42 | 17 | 42 | 17 | 42 | | |
| 18 | 43 | 18 | 43 | 18 | 43 | 18 | 43 | | |
| 19 | 44 | 19 | 44 | 19 | 44 | 19 | 44 | | |
| 20 | 45 | 20 | 45 | 20 | 45 | 20 | 45 | | |
| 21 | 46 | 21 | 46 | 21 | 46 | 21 | 46 | | |
| 22 | 47 | 22 | 47 | 22 | 47 | 22 | 47 | | |
| 23 | 48 | 23 | 48 | 23 | 48 | 23 | 48 | | |
| 24 | 49 | 24 | 49 | 24 | 49 | 24 | 49 | | |
| 25 | 50 | 25 | 50 | 25 | 50 | 25 | 50 | | |
| ___ x 1 = ___ | | ___ x 2 = ___ | | ___ x 3 = ___ | | ___ x 4 = ___ | | ___ x 4 = ___ | |

Multiply total number correct by point value/quarter to calculate totals for each quarter.
Add total of all quarters below.
**Total Points:** _____

Thank you for playing ***Orangeology Trivia Challenge***.

**Additional score sheets are available at:
www.TriviaGameBooks.com**

# Player / Team Score Sheet

Name:_____

| Preseason | | Regular Season | | Conference Tournament | | Championship Game | | Overtime Bonus | |
|---|---|---|---|---|---|---|---|---|---|
| 1 | 26 | 1 | 26 | 1 | 26 | 1 | 26 | 1 | |
| 2 | 27 | 2 | 27 | 2 | 27 | 2 | 27 | 2 | |
| 3 | 28 | 3 | 28 | 3 | 28 | 3 | 28 | 3 | |
| 4 | 29 | 4 | 29 | 4 | 29 | 4 | 29 | 4 | |
| 5 | 30 | 5 | 30 | 5 | 30 | 5 | 30 | 5 | |
| 6 | 31 | 6 | 31 | 6 | 31 | 6 | 31 | 6 | |
| 7 | 32 | 7 | 32 | 7 | 32 | 7 | 32 | 7 | |
| 8 | 33 | 8 | 33 | 8 | 33 | 8 | 33 | 8 | |
| 9 | 34 | 9 | 34 | 9 | 34 | 9 | 34 | 9 | |
| 10 | 35 | 10 | 35 | 10 | 35 | 10 | 35 | 10 | |
| 11 | 36 | 11 | 36 | 11 | 36 | 11 | 36 | | |
| 12 | 37 | 12 | 37 | 12 | 37 | 12 | 37 | | |
| 13 | 38 | 13 | 38 | 13 | 38 | 13 | 38 | | |
| 14 | 39 | 14 | 39 | 14 | 39 | 14 | 39 | | |
| 15 | 40 | 15 | 40 | 15 | 40 | 15 | 40 | | |
| 16 | 41 | 16 | 41 | 16 | 41 | 16 | 41 | | |
| 17 | 42 | 17 | 42 | 17 | 42 | 17 | 42 | | |
| 18 | 43 | 18 | 43 | 18 | 43 | 18 | 43 | | |
| 19 | 44 | 19 | 44 | 19 | 44 | 19 | 44 | | |
| 20 | 45 | 20 | 45 | 20 | 45 | 20 | 45 | | |
| 21 | 46 | 21 | 46 | 21 | 46 | 21 | 46 | | |
| 22 | 47 | 22 | 47 | 22 | 47 | 22 | 47 | | |
| 23 | 48 | 23 | 48 | 23 | 48 | 23 | 48 | | |
| 24 | 49 | 24 | 49 | 24 | 49 | 24 | 49 | | |
| 25 | 50 | 25 | 50 | 25 | 50 | 25 | 50 | | |

____ x 1 = ____    ____ x 2 = ____    ____ x 3 = ____    ____ x 4 = ____    ____ x 4 = ____

Multiply total number correct by point value/quarter to calculate totals for each quarter.

Add total of all quarters below.

**Total Points:_____**

Thank you for playing *Orangeology Trivia Challenge*.

**Additional score sheets are available at:**
**www.TriviaGameBooks.com**